Wilma
RUDOLPH

WILMA RUDOLPH

by Jennifer Joline Anderson

ABDO
Publishing Company

Content Consultant: Yvon Morris
Sports Information, Archives Coordinator
Tennessee State University

Published by ABDO Publishing Company, 8000 West 78th Street, Edina, Minnesota 55439. Copyright © 2011 by Abdo Consulting Group, Inc. International copyrights reserved in all countries. No part of this book may be reproduced in any form without written permission from the publisher. SportsZone™ is a trademark and logo of ABDO Publishing Company.

Printed in the United States of America,
North Mankato, Minnesota
112010
012011

 THIS BOOK CONTAINS AT LEAST 10% RECYCLED MATERIALS.

Editor: Matt Tustison
Copy Editor: Paula Lewis
Series Design: Christa Schneider
Cover Production: Christa Schneider
Interior Production: Sarah Carlson and Carol Castro

Library of Congress Cataloging-in-Publication Data
Anderson, Jennifer Joline.
  Wilma Rudolph : track and field inspiration / by Jennifer Joline Anderson.
    p. cm. — (Legendary athletes)
  Includes bibliographical references and index.
  ISBN 978-1-61714-759-3
  1. Rudolph, Wilma, 1940—-Juvenile literature. 2. Runners (Sports)—United States—Biography—Juvenile literature. 3. Women runners—United States—Biography—Juvenile literature. I. Title.
  GV1061.15.R83A53 2011
  796.42092—dc22
  [B]
                              2010046698

TABLE OF CONTENTS

CHAPTER 1	The Fastest Woman on Earth	6
CHAPTER 2	Beating the Odds	14
CHAPTER 3	Becoming an Athlete	24
CHAPTER 4	Toughening Up	34
CHAPTER 5	To the Olympics	44
CHAPTER 6	Challenge and Change	56
CHAPTER 7	Going for Gold	64
CHAPTER 8	A Sweet Taste	76
CHAPTER 9	Life after Track	86
	Timeline	96
	Essential Facts	100
	Glossary	102
	Additional Resources	104
	Source Notes	106
	Index	110
	About the Author	112

CHAPTER 1

Wilma Rudolph competed in the 1960 Olympics in Rome, Italy. Rudolph had also raced in the Olympics in 1956, but by 1960, at age 20, she was faster than ever.

The Fastest Woman on Earth

The coach was certain something was wrong. The track must be short, or the clock must be off. The time he witnessed could not be right. In his years coaching women's track and field at Tennessee A&I State University, Ed Temple had never seen any woman run as fast as Wilma Rudolph. Nobody had. Right before his eyes, the slender, brown-skinned 20-year-old had broken a world record. The fastest any woman had ever run the 200-meter dash was 24.1 seconds, and Rudolph had done it in 22.9.

The year was 1960, and Coach Temple had been training his team, the Tigerbelles, to try out for the Summer Olympics, to be held in Rome, Italy. Rudolph's time in this race more than qualified her for the Olympics. If the time were correct, she would be the fastest woman in the Olympics.

Coach Temple shook his head in disbelief. He remembered discovering Wilma at a basketball game when she was a skinny tenth grader.

Back then, he had not seen anything really outstanding about her, but with her long legs and raw speed, he thought she had potential. During the past four years, though, Rudolph had trained hard. She had learned all the techniques of running. Now she was a world-class sprinter, and Coach Temple was immensely proud. But when Rudolph came back and sat down after the race, he did not make a fuss. It was not his style. Instead he only smiled and said, "Doin' all right, aren't you?"[1]

High Olympic Hopes

Rudolph was definitely doing all right. With the new time, she knew she would easily make the Olympic team. She had already competed in the Olympics once before, in Melbourne, Australia, in 1956. Back then, she had been only 16, and she and her teammates

"She ran like a gazelle. She was so beautiful. And once she started working with her arms, and starting the legs together, and the feet together, and the leaning, then the confidence came automatically and you couldn't beat her. You couldn't come close to her."[2]

—Barbara Jones, a friend and teammate of Wilma's at Tennessee A&I State University

captured a bronze medal in the 4x100-meter relay. Four years had passed, and Rudolph was faster than ever. This time, she planned to win the gold.

Rudolph's goal was to win not one but three gold medals in three different sprint events: the 100-meter dash, the 200-meter run, and the 4x100-meter relay. If she succeeded, she would establish an Olympic record for American women runners. Rudolph's hero was Jesse Owens, the legendary African-American sprinter

History of the Olympics

The original Olympic Games were held in the city of Olympia, Greece, in ancient times. Greece was then divided into city-states, and they often warred against one another. The Games were a way of coming together in a peaceful way. The original Games featured only male athletes, who competed naked. Women were not allowed to participate or watch the Olympic Games. The Games stopped being held at the end of the fourth century AD.

In the late 1800s, French historian Baron Pierre de Coubertin had the idea of starting the Olympics again. In 1896, the first modern Olympic Games were held in Athens, Greece. The athletes wore clothes. Women did not compete until the second Olympics, in 1900 in Paris, France. The first Winter Olympics were held in 1924 to feature sporting events that could not be held in summer. The Summer Games have been held every four years in different locations around the world since 1896, except in 1916, 1940, and 1944, when the Games were canceled because of war. The 1940 and 1944 Winter Games were also canceled because of war.

The Olympics are a symbol of international peace and cooperation, as they allow amateur athletes of all nations to compete in a nonpolitical setting.

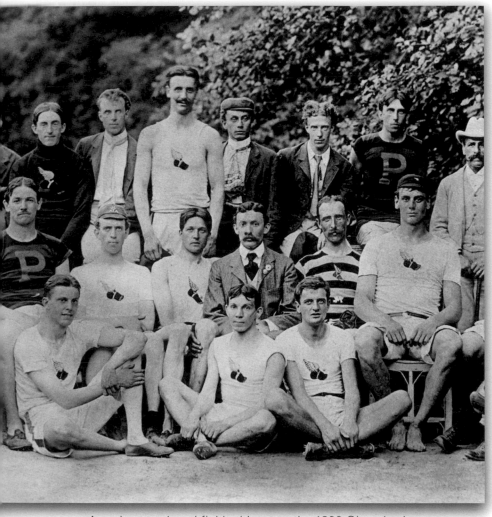

American track and field athletes at the 1900 Olympics in Paris, France

who had won four gold medals in the 1936 Olympic Games. She wanted her performance at the Olympics to be a tribute to him.

At the 1960 Olympic trials in Abilene, Texas, Rudolph tried out for the sprint events, easily qualifying for all three. It was at the trials that she ran the 200-meter dash in 22.9 seconds, setting the world record.

Rudolph was thrilled she had qualified for the Olympics along with three of her Tennessee State teammates. Just before leaving Texas, Rudolph got more great news. Coach Temple had been selected to coach the women's track team at the Olympics. He would be going with his Tigerbelles to Rome. Rudolph was overjoyed. She recollected in her autobiography,

> My own coach, the one who stuck with me through thick and thin, was going to be the Olympic coach.[3] . . . I knew there was a good chance to win three gold medals in Rome, and I knew if I didn't win three, it would be my fault alone. Everything was in place for me.[4]

Rudolph was nearly six feet (1.83 m) tall. She ran

Olympic Sprint Events

The Olympic sprint events include the 100-meter dash, the 200-meter dash, the 400-meter dash, and the 4x100- and 4x400-meter relays. One lap around the track is 400 meters. One half of the track is 200 meters. It includes one length of the track plus one curve. The distance of one length of the track, not counting any part of the curve, is 100 meters.

Jesse Owens

Jesse Owens, an African-American sprinter from Alabama, was the hero of the 1936 Olympics in Berlin, Germany, and a hero to Wilma Rudolph. At the time, Adolf Hitler led the Nazi Party and Germany. Hitler believed that his blond-haired, blue-eyed German athletes were part of a superior Aryan race, and he saw the Olympics as a chance to prove it to the world. But Owens humiliated Hitler when he beat the German runners, taking home four gold medals, one each for the 100-meter dash, the 200-meter dash, the long jump, and the 4x100-meter relay. Owens set Olympic records in the 200-meter dash and the long jump. His relay team broke a world record.

with long, powerful strides and carried herself with confidence. To anyone who saw her, Rudolph looked as though she had been born to win. But in fact, it had been a long road to get here. Rudolph had been crippled by polio as a child, and the doctors said she would never be able to walk again. It was almost a miracle that she had become what she was—a world-class Olympic athlete.

Jesse Owens, shown in 1933, was Rudolph's idol because he won four gold medals in the 1936 Olympics.

CHAPTER 2

Wilma's older sister Yvonne, *left*, and six-year-old Wilma, *right*

Beating the Odds

When Wilma Glodean Rudolph was small, her family never imagined that she would grow up to become a world-record-breaking track star. They were not even sure if she would grow up at all. At her birth on June 23, 1940, in St. Bethlehem, Tennessee, Wilma weighed only four and one-half pounds (2 kg). Born two months early, she was not expected to live. Baby Wilma surprised everyone when she lived beyond the first few days. She was a survivor.

Being a premature baby was only the first of Wilma's challenges. Tiny and weak during the first few years of her life, she also contracted measles, whooping cough, and chicken pox. The Rudolphs did not have much money to pay a doctor. Besides, southern states such as Tennessee were racially segregated, and African Americans could not get treatment in white hospitals or clinics. There was only one black physician, Dr. Coleman, who served the black community. Wilma's mother,

Childhood Vaccinations

Beginning in the 1940s and 1950s, vaccines were introduced to immunize children from common infectious diseases such as the measles, mumps, whooping cough, and polio. Vaccines work by infecting the body with a weak or dead version of the bacteria or virus that causes the disease. The bacteria or virus in the vaccine is not strong enough to cause the person to become sick. But it alerts the body's immune system to create antibodies that can fight the disease. Then, if the vaccinated person comes into contact with the disease later on, the body can fight it off. Unfortunately, vaccines were not yet available when Wilma was a child.

Blanche Rudolph, treated Wilma at home, calling on the doctor only in emergencies.

My mother used to have all these home remedies she would make herself, and I lived on them. She was very big on hot toddys. That was a concoction of liquor, corn, sugar and a few things that she would cook on the stove. . . . Another thing my mother was big on was making me sweat. She would pile blanket on top of blanket and make me get under them and sweat.[1]

When Wilma was four, she became gravely ill with double pneumonia and then scarlet fever. Today, these deadly infections can be fought with antibiotic medicine. But in the early 1940s, antibiotics were not widely available. For weeks, Wilma lay near death. When she recovered, her family noticed that Wilma's left leg had become crippled. It was crooked, and her foot turned inward. Wilma had been infected with polio, a virus that attacks the nervous system and muscles.

Doctors recommended massage and physical therapy to strengthen Wilma's leg, but they warned that Wilma would probably never walk again.

Twentieth of 22

Luckily for Wilma, she had a family who believed in her—and a big family, at that. Wilma was the twentieth of 22 children. Her father, Ed Rudolph, had 11 children by his first marriage and 11 with Wilma's mother, Blanche. By the time Wilma was born, most of the older children had moved out. But there were still five young children living at home, and the others came around

A Dreaded Childhood Disease

Poliomyelitis, or polio, is caused by a virus that is spread by human-to-human contact. About 90 percent of the time, the virus causes no symptoms. But in a few cases, it damages the central nervous system, leaving patients with crippled arms or legs. Or worse, the muscles that control eating and breathing can be affected, leading to death.

From the 1880s to the 1950s, polio epidemics swept the world. Tens of thousands of Americans, mostly young children, were paralyzed or killed by the disease. Across the United States, treatment centers were set up to care for polio patients. The treatment involved massaging the muscles and soaking in hot baths. In hospitals, machines called iron lungs helped patients who could not breathe on their own.

There is no cure for polio, but vaccines to prevent the disease were developed by Jonas Salk in 1952 and Albert Sabin in 1961. The vaccines wiped out polio in the United States. No polio cases have been reported in the country since 1999.

often. With such a large family, there were plenty of helping hands. Wilma's brothers and sisters took turns massaging her leg four times each day as part of her therapy.

In the early 1940s, the United States was still coming out of the Great Depression, and the Rudolphs had to scrape to get by. Ed Rudolph worked as a railroad porter and handyman while Wilma's mother labored as a housemaid for white families. Their incomes only added up to approximately $2,500 each year. Wilma felt sorry that her mother had to work so hard for little money. "The way my mother worked, somebody should have been serving her coffee in bed on Saturday mornings. Instead, she did the serving."[2]

Shortly after Wilma was born, the family moved to a house in a black neighborhood of Clarksville, Tennessee. The home had few of the comforts people enjoy today. There was no indoor plumbing or electricity, so the family had their toilet in an outhouse and used kerosene lamps and candles for light. Although money was tight, Wilma's parents refused to accept government welfare. "We didn't have too much money back then," Wilma recalled, "but we had everything else, especially love."[3]

"The doctors told me I would never walk, but my mother told me I would, so I believed in my mother."[4]
—Wilma Rudolph

A Nashville, Tennessee, segregation sign from the 1950s transit system

Although doctors thought it unlikely that Wilma's leg could be cured, Wilma's mother was determined to try everything to help her daughter. Twice a week, beginning when Wilma was six, Wilma and her mother traveled an hour by bus to Nashville. There, Wilma received treatment at a black hospital at Meharry Medical College. The treatment involved painful exercises, stretching, massage, and soaking in a hot whirlpool bath. Wilma hated to put her leg into the

Racial Segregation in the South

When Wilma was a child, racial segregation was the law throughout much of the southern United States. Black people were not permitted to drink from the same water fountains, use the same bathrooms, or eat in the same restaurants as whites. They could not attend the same schools or be treated at the same hospitals.

When they rode the Greyhound bus to Nashville, Wilma and her mother had to sit at the back. They carried a lunch because there were no restaurants near the bus station that would serve black customers. Despite the negative experience of segregation, the bus rides were good for Wilma. They allowed her to see the world outside her small town of Clarksville, and she began to dream of a different future for herself.

steaming hot water, but her mother reminded her, "Wilma, the key element here is not the water, it's the heat."[5] Wilma doubted the treatment was working, but she obeyed her mother.

Different from the Others

Because Wilma could not walk, she was unable to go to school with the other children. She wore a heavy metal brace to straighten her crooked leg and a heavy brown orthopedic shoe made to support her foot. The brace and shoe marked her as different from the others. When Wilma went outside to play, other kids taunted her, calling her a "cripple." Her brothers and sisters stuck up for Wilma, but the teasing still made her sad and angry. She vowed that some day others would not only accept her but admire her.

I remember the kids always saying, "I don't want to play with her. We don't want her on our team." So I never had a chance to participate. And all my young life I would say, "One day I'm going to be somebody very special. And I'm not going to forget those kids."[6]

While trying to fit in, Wilma sometimes took off her brace in secret, practicing walking without it. Outside the house, she would try hard to walk without a limp, hoping others would think her leg was improving. Although she did not know it, this was helping her leg grow stronger. By the second grade, she was strong enough to start attending school at Cobb Elementary. Entering school marked a new beginning for Wilma. "I went from being a sickly kid the other kids teased to a normal person accepted by her peer group. . . . I needed to belong, and I finally did."[7]

What Are You Doing with *Him*?

During Wilma's childhood, some whites considered it wrong for the races to mix. With her reddish hair and light brown skin, Wilma did not look as black as her siblings. Sometimes white people would see her with her darker-skinned brother, Wesley, and ask, "Little girl, what are you doing walking with *him?*"[8]

Walking Tall

When she was nine and one-half years old, Wilma took off her brace in public for the first time. She walked proudly down the aisle at church, allowing friends and neighbors to see her without the brace. Looking back, Wilma remembered:

> It was one of the most important moments of my life. From that day on, people were going to start separating me from that brace, start thinking about me differently, start saying that Wilma is a healthy kid, just like all the rest of them.[9]

Wilma still needed to wear the brace for a few more years. But when she was 12, the day came when her mother packed up the hated brace and sent it back to the hospital in Nashville.

"After the scarlet fever and the whooping cough, I remember I started to get mad about it all. . . . I think I started acquiring a competitive spirit right then and there, a spirit that would make me successful in sports later on. I was mad, and I was going to beat these illnesses no matter what."[10]

—*Wilma Rudolph*

Wilma had beaten all the odds. When doctors did not think she could live more than a day, she had survived. She had battled deadly illnesses and won. And now, through sheer determination, she had amazed the doctors by learning to walk again. But Wilma was not satisfied with being able to walk. She had her heart set on becoming an athlete.

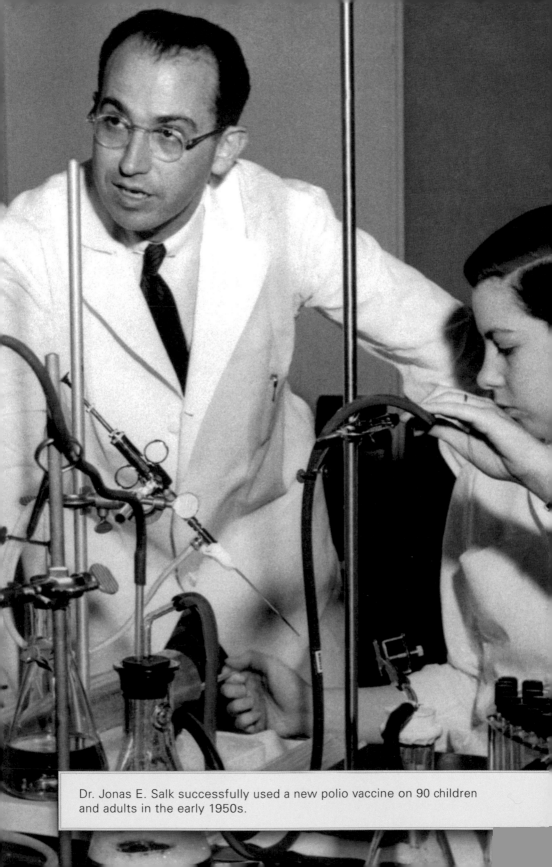

Dr. Jonas E. Salk successfully used a new polio vaccine on 90 children and adults in the early 1950s.

Wilma, who was a standout in basketball, picked up track and field quickly and became a star in that sport as well at Burt High School.

Becoming an Athlete

Wilma Rudolph's first love in sports was not track, but basketball. As a young child, she had watched while the neighborhood kids played. The kids lacked the right equipment. They would play with whatever balls they could find—beach balls, rubber balls, or even tennis balls. They used old peach baskets with the bottoms broken out and put them on poles in someone's backyard. Wilma liked the fact that she did not have to run very much to play basketball. She could just stand in one spot and wait for the ball to come to her.

But Wilma's mother did not approve of her playing basketball. She worried that Wilma would injure herself. And, in those days, sports were seen as unladylike. Wilma remembered:

> *Down South, there was the old "ladies-don't-do-such-things" way of thinking. You couldn't be a lady and a good athlete at the same time. There was a lot of talk about "playing sports will give you muscles, and you'll look just like*

a man." They would say, "If you run around too much as a girl you'll never be able to have children." . . . *I hated all that and always knew, deep down, that it was a bunch of nonsense. But over half of the girls in the school believed that stuff. . . . They had this terrible fear that the boys in school just wouldn't look at them if they were athletes.*[1]

Wilma's father did not object to her playing, though, and eventually her mother relaxed and allowed it too. When Wilma was in the seventh grade, she tried out for the Burt High School girls basketball team coached by Clinton Gray. He allowed Wilma to join because her sister Yvonne was already on the team. But although Wilma tried hard to impress Coach Gray, he did not think she was good enough to play in any games.

Wilma sat on the bench for two seasons. While she sat, she watched closely. She noticed how people dribbled the ball, how they passed, and how they drew fouls while shooting in order to get free throws. Wilma practiced stealing the ball, shooting, and rebounding.

Sexism in Sports

Until the 1960s and 1970s, many American high schools did not have strong athletic programs for female students. The boys teams received most of the funds because they were considered to be more important. In 1972, the US government issued an education law called Title IX. The law states that schools cannot discriminate on the basis of sex. Today, there are a wide range of sports opportunities for young women.

By the ninth grade, she thought she was as good or better than most girls on the team. But Coach Gray still ignored her, and it made her mad. She became more determined than ever that somehow, she was going to have her chance.

At the end of the basketball season that year, Coach Gray started a new sport at the school. It was girls track and field. He saw it mostly as a way to keep his players in shape during the off-season. Wilma quickly found that she loved running. "Running . . . was nothing but pure enjoyment for me," she recalled. "I was doing it all on natural ability, and I had no idea about the technical aspects of the sport," she admitted.[2] She did not know how to warm up properly or to work her breathing. She had a lot to learn about running. And she still loved basketball more. But Wilma won every race she ran that season. She started to think that track could be her true sport.

"When I was running, I had the sense of freedom, of running in the wind. I never forgot all the years when I was a little girl and not able to be involved. When I ran, I felt like a butterfly. That feeling was always there."[3]

—*Wilma Rudolph*

Getting Noticed

When Wilma reached the tenth grade, she was nearly six feet (1.83 m) tall. With her height and reach, she decided this was the year she would start playing some real basketball. One evening just before the start of the new season, Wilma and her friend Nancy Bowen practiced one-on-one in the gym, making sure Coach Gray was watching. The coach did not say anything, but at the first game, he tagged Wilma and Nancy to start. Wilma was thrilled. She was finally noticed.

Wilma started at the position of guard that season and quickly became a star. In one game, played before the entire school, Wilma scored 32 points. She did not miss a shot. The girl who had once been teased as "crippled" was now a school sports hero. "That was very important to me," Wilma wrote, "getting the recognition and the attention from my own peers."[4]

But although Wilma was doing well, Coach Gray was hard on her and often yelled when she made a mistake. She hated being yelled at, and sometimes quit the team, only to play again the next day. However angry she got, she admired Coach Gray and his dedication to the team.

Skeeter

While playing for Coach Gray's basketball team, Wilma earned a new nickname. Coach Gray called her Skeeter because she had long, skinny arms and legs and was always buzzing around him like a mosquito. Soon, all of Wilma's friends knew her as Skeeter.

The Taste of Defeat

That year, the girls basketball team beat all the teams in its conference. The team went on to the state tournament, hoping to prevail as the best in Tennessee. The team won its first game with Wilma scoring 26 points. But in the second game, the girls made a lot of mistakes and lost. The tournament was over for them. The girls cried in the locker room. They were heartbroken—how could they lose?

Segregation in Schools

Until the 1950s, schools in the southern United States were segregated by law. Black students were prohibited from attending white schools. Sporting events such as basketball games and track meets were also segregated—black students and white students rarely had a chance to mix.

Wilma Rudolph attended the black schools in Clarksville: Cobb Elementary and Burt High. Although black and white schools were supposed to be separate but equal, that often was not the case. Black schools received fewer funds from the government and often lacked supplies and equipment. Teachers in black schools were paid far less.

In the mid-1950s, when Wilma was in high school, the law changed. The US Supreme Court decided in the case *Brown v. Board of Education* that racial segregation of schools was unfair to black students. It became illegal to segregate public schools. But some southern states ignored the ruling for several years.

In 1957, Arkansas Governor Orval Faubus called out the National Guard to prevent black students from entering Little Rock Central High School. President Dwight Eisenhower responded, sending troops to Little Rock to escort the black students into the school. It was a landmark moment for the Civil Rights Movement.

An African-American student at Little Rock Central High is escorted to an army station wagon to return home after class in 1957.

With the basketball season over, Wilma threw herself into track. She even cut classes to run until she got in trouble with the principal for it. Wilma was still winning every race she ran.

Then came the big track meet of the year in the spring of 1956. It was called the Amateur Athletic Union (AAU) contest. The meet was held at Tuskegee Institute, an all-black college in Alabama, and girls from all over the South were invited to compete. Coach Gray warned that the competition would be tough, but Wilma was not worried. "I was a little cocky . . . because, after all, I had won every single race I had ever been in up to that point," she recalled later.[5] She thought she could beat anyone. Instead, she lost. Wilma did not win a single race that day, nor did she qualify for anything. She was crushed.

It was a difficult lesson for Wilma, but one that she would carry the rest of her life. She had learned to love the taste of winning, but sometimes, she

First Love

While Wilma was getting noticed in sports, she was getting noticed by boys too. One boy, Robert Eldridge, became her first love. She had known Robert since they were kids, when he used to throw rocks to get her attention. Now the two dated steadily.

"Winning is great, sure, but if you are really going to do something in life, the secret is learning how to lose. Nobody goes undefeated all the time. If you can pick up after a crushing defeat, and go on to win again, you are going to be a champion someday."[6]

—*Wilma Rudolph*

had to experience the bitter taste of defeat.

But all was not lost at Tuskegee. Watching the meet that day was Ed Temple, the coach of the famous Tigerbelles, the women's track team at Tennessee State University in Nashville. Temple had seen Wilma when she had played basketball in the state tournament. He was always looking for young talent to recruit for his team. It was clear that 15-year-old Wilma had talent.

Temple invited Wilma to attend a summer track and field training camp at Tennessee State. There, she would train with high school and university students and learn the techniques of running. Wilma welcomed the opportunity. Tuskegee had taught her that she could not win on talent alone—she had to develop skills if she wanted to be a champion.

In 1957, nine black students were refused admittance to Little Rock Central High School by Arkansas National Guardsmen, as ordered by Governor Orval Faubus.

CHAPTER 4

Willye White, shown here in 1964, trained with Wilma Rudolph beginning in 1956 and had a successful track career of her own.

Toughening Up

In the summer of 1956, Wilma Rudolph turned 16 and went to Nashville to train with one of the finest women's track teams in the nation, the Tennessee State University (TSU) Tigerbelles. At first, Wilma's parents did not want her to go. They thought she was too young. But Wilma's coach, Ed Temple, convinced them he would take good care of her. All expenses would be paid for by the university, and if she did well enough, she might win a scholarship to TSU when she finished high school.

Wilma's parents knew it was an opportunity she could not afford to miss. "You're the first one in this house that ever had a chance to go to college," her mother said. "If running's going to do that, I just want you to set your mind to be the best!"[1]

The first two weeks of the camp were especially tough. Coach Temple had the runners on a long-distance routine designed to improve their endurance. They ran six miles (9.66 km)

"We had to run up and down hills, and we had to run through mud, and we had to get up at five o'clock in the morning. Because [Coach Temple] felt that if you could get up at five in the morning, if you could run in the Tennessee sun at twelve o'clock noon, if you could run in the evening at five in the rain, then nothing could stop you."[3]
—*Barbara Jones, one of the Tigerbelles*

in the morning, in the middle of the day, and again in the late afternoon. After the long-distance training was over, Coach Temple focused on some of the important basics of running. Wilma learned to relax her body while running by breathing properly and keeping her hands loose. Relaxing was important for Wilma because she would become very tense before a race. "I would get this horrible feeling in the pit of my stomach," Wilma explained. "Sometimes, I would vomit, or get this vomiting feeling. This form of tension stayed with me my entire career."[2]

Another difficulty Wilma had was with the starting blocks used in sprint races. Runners use the blocks to help them push off at the beginning of a race. But Wilma had such long legs that she was never comfortable crunched down onto the blocks.

Also, she had bad reflexes. Because of this, it took her longer to get started once the gun went off. "I would come out and I'd be wobbling, and my first five or six strides would always be off," she remembered.[4] Because her starts were bad, Wilma did not run well in shorter sprints such as the 50-meter dash. She preferred the 100-meter and 200-meter dashes, which gave her time to catch up to the other runners. After a slow start, she could pick up speed and blast to the front. Wilma's challenges taught her a new lesson: "Every runner is different, and every runner has different problems."[5]

The hardest challenge for Wilma was learning to compete against the other runners. As one of the youngest at the training camp, Wilma sometimes held back and allowed the older, more

Running Tips from Wilma Rudolph

While training with Coach Temple, Wilma learned important basics of running. She lists some tips in her autobiography: "[Keep] the fists loose. . . . The less tense your muscles are, the better you can run. . . . Run with open hands and, chances are, the rest of you is just as loose.

"[Don't run] while leaning backwards. . . . You've got to lean into your race, not away from it."

Before a race, "[take] long, deep breaths, take air in and let it out; doing this a couple of times relaxes everything."[6]

experienced girls to win. She was afraid they would not like or accept her if she beat them. But if she was going to reach her full potential as a runner, Wilma had to toughen up—not only physically, but mentally. She had to stop trying to be liked and start trying to win.

A New Goal

Coach Temple put together a junior relay team with Wilma and three other younger girls, Martha Hudson, Willye White, and Annette Anderson. The team ran the 440-meter relay. Each girl ran 110 meters, passing a

Nation's Best: the Tigerbelles

Ed Temple was head coach of TSU's women's track team, the Tigerbelles, for 44 years before retiring in 1994. TSU is a historically black university, and the Tigerbelles were an African-American team. But under Temple's leadership, the Tigerbelles became the best track team in the nation—black or white. Coach Temple led the Tigerbelles to 34 national titles, 23 Olympic medals, and 30 medals in the Pan American Games.

Approximately 90 percent of the high school girls who participated in Temple's summer track camp ended up attending TSU. Wilma Rudolph was one of them, earning her degree there in 1963. Today, along with other historically black colleges and universities in the United States, TSU admits students of all ethnic backgrounds. African Americans make up approximately 74 percent of the student population, while 22 percent of the students are white. Latinos, Asians, and students of other ethnicities also attend the school.

stick, or baton, to the next runner as she completed her leg of the race. Wilma tried running all four different legs of the relay. Because of her slow starts, she did not like to go first. She preferred to run the final, or anchor, leg of the relay. When the team was behind, she knew she could run fast enough to pull ahead and win.

The team practiced running relays over and over. The runners worked hard at passing the baton. That was an important skill because the handoff had to be fast and smooth so that no time was lost. Since the receiver could not look back to see where the baton was, it was the responsibility of the passer to make sure the receiver got it firmly in hand. If the baton was dropped in the middle of the race, the team was automatically disqualified.

Coach Temple rarely praised the runners. "He never said very much," Wilma remembered. "We found out if he didn't say anything, you were doing all right. If he started saying things to you, that usually meant you were in trouble."[7] So, even if their coach did not say so, the girls knew they were doing very well. They were excited for the next big track event, the national AAU meet in Philadelphia, Pennsylvania. This time, girls all over the United States would be competing. Wilma and the others on the junior relay team had a new goal: to win at the AAU meet.

Coach Temple's Rules

Coach Temple had strict rules for the girls in his training camp. They included:
- Be in by 9:00 each night.
- No riding in cars.
- No going into night-clubs.

Still, the Tigerbelles had fun over the summer. They amused themselves by playing a card game called Bid-Wist. Wilma's boyfriend, Robert Eldridge, came to visit on weekends, and so did her brothers and sisters and her high school coach, Coach Gray.

Winning in Philadelphia

The team traveled by a caravan of cars to the AAU track meet in Philadelphia. In her autobiography, Wilma described her reaction to the vast northern city:

Everything in Philadelphia seemed so foreign to me; the buildings seemed so big, so awesome, I was intimidated. When we went to the stadium—Franklin Field—I nearly fainted. I had never seen a stadium that big before.[8]

Wilma and the other high school age girls ran in the junior division of the AAU meet, and just as they had hoped, they won big. Their 440-meter relay team won three times that day—twice in the qualifying heats and once in the final race. Wilma also ran the 75-meter dash and the 100-meter dash, winning the qualifying races and the finals. That made nine races Wilma ran that day, and she won them all. TSU went home with the junior title of the AAU meet.

Although it was an impressive victory, none of the girls expected recognition for it. "I won nine races that day, and our team won the junior title, and none of us even thought about looking in the sports pages the next day . . . because we knew automatically that nobody would bother to write us up," Wilma remembered. "It was like, oh, well, girls' track, that's not really a sports event."[9]

Female runners at that time were not as respected in the United States as they are today. But although Wilma did not know it then, she was destined to change that in just a few years when her accomplishments as a sprinter brought her onto the world stage.

Heats at a Track Meet

At a track meet, runners first participate in a series of heats, or qualifying races. The winners of the first qualifying heats go on to run semifinal heats. Those few who win the semifinals go on to the final race. At the AAU track meet, Wilma won the qualifying heats and the semifinal heats and went on to victory in the finals.

Jackie Robinson

Jackie Robinson made history when he became the first African American to play major league baseball since the 1880s. Before he joined the Brooklyn Dodgers in 1947, blacks had been banned from the big leagues for 60 years. Robinson broke the color barrier, putting an end to the racial segregation in baseball. Although many regarded him as a hero, Robinson had to endure racist insults from angry fans and even other baseball players. But he continued on and became one of the top players in the majors. When Wilma met Robinson in 1956, he had just retired from baseball and was an international celebrity.

Meeting a Hero

At the AAU meet, the girls from TSU had a chance to meet two African-American baseball stars, Don Newcombe and Jackie Robinson. Wilma was too shy to speak to them. She felt embarrassed by her strong southern accent. But to her surprise, Robinson spoke first. He had been watching the meet, and he was impressed. "I really like your style of running," he said, "and I really think you have a lot of potential. . . . Don't let anything, or anybody, keep you from running."[10]

Jackie Robinson of the Brooklyn Dodgers in 1956

CHAPTER 5

Mae Faggs, *right*, and Wilma Rudolph, *left*, finished in a tie in the 200-meter dash at the 1956 US Olympic trials.

To the Olympics

While Wilma Rudolph was growing up in Tennessee, she had never heard much about the Olympics. When her coach, Ed Temple, asked her to try out for the Olympic track team in the summer of 1956, she did not really know what the Olympics were. She assumed it was no big deal—just another track meet.

But as she soon found out, the Olympics were a very big deal. If Wilma could make the team, she would compete alongside the finest amateur athletes in the world in Melbourne, Australia.

Before she knew it, Wilma was piling into a station wagon with Coach Temple and five girls from the Tigerbelles track team. They were on their way across the country to Seattle, Washington, to compete in the Olympic trials.

Little Mae and Skeeter

At 16, Wilma was the youngest of the group. As her teammate Isabelle Daniels remembered, "We all had to see about Skeeter."[1] The star of the team, Mae Faggs, helped Wilma the most. Faggs, known as "Little Mae," was only five feet, two inches (1.57 m) tall, but she was a powerful runner. Faggs had been to the Olympics twice, taking home a gold medal in 1952 for the 4x100-meter relay. It was Faggs who taught Rudolph what the Olympics really were. She explained that the five interlocking rings on the Olympic logo stood for the five parts of the world—North America and South America, Europe, Africa, Asia, and Australia—that come together every four years to compete in the Games.

Faggs was like a second coach to Wilma. She saw that Wilma was holding herself back, letting the older girls win because she wanted to be liked. She encouraged Wilma not to worry about fitting in with anyone else but to try to succeed as an individual. Now was Wilma's time to excel.

It was good advice, but while getting ready for the 200-meter trials, Wilma was nervous. The weather was very cold in Seattle, and she was used to running in the heat of Tennessee. The stadium was huge, and as many as 60 girls were trying to make the team. Wilma got the familiar sick feeling in her stomach. She did not know whether she could do it.

Only the top three runners in the race would qualify for the Olympic team. Faggs knew she could take first. She thought maybe Wilma could take second or third. "Skeeter Baby," Faggs said, "you want to make the United States Olympic Team? All you have to do to make this team is stick with me. . . . You stick with me in the race, you make the team."[3]

Off the Track

Wilma was fast on the track but slow off it. Her favorite hobby, according to her Olympic teammates in 1960, was sleeping. "Next to that, it's reading, mostly in bed," added her teammate Martha Hudson.[4]

A Dead Heat

The runners crouched in the starting blocks before the 200-meter trial, Faggs in the inside lane and Wilma right next to her. When the starting gun went off, they leapt out of the blocks and strode into the curve. Faggs was out in front, moving fast. But as they came to the straightaway, Wilma pulled up beside Faggs. She stayed right on her shoulder until they reached the tape. They finished in a dead heat, or an even tie, for first place.

Coach Temple walked up to congratulate his two star runners as they stopped to catch their breath. Faggs laughed and shouted to Wilma, "Now look, fool, I told you to stay on my shoulder. I didn't tell you to act like you wanted to pass me!"[5]

Actually, Faggs was delighted that her young teammate had done so well. She told Wilma a secret:

> You know, as soon as this thing is over, I'm going to retire. I think you've made it, you're ready to replace me right now. You really beat me in that race. What took you so long to get there? We've all known you had it in you, but we all wondered when it would come out. Today it did.[6]

From then on, Wilma always did her best.

Going to Melbourne

The Summer Olympics were being held that year in Melbourne, Australia—half a world away from

Clarksville, Tennessee. Wilma learned that because Australia was in the Southern Hemisphere, its seasons were opposite of those at home. The Games were scheduled for November and December, which was springtime in Australia.

Twenty girls would take part in the US women's Olympic track team. Incredibly, six of them were from Coach Temple's program at Tennessee State. It was the first time any university had sent so many runners to the Olympic Games. On their way to the Olympics, the team stopped in Los Angeles, California, to participate in a two-week training camp.

Wilma had never been on an airplane before. When the flight attendant asked what she would like to eat, she said, "Nothing." She thought she would have to pay for the food, and she did not have any money for such things. Faggs quietly told her that the meal was free, and she accepted it. But even then, Wilma could not eat a bite. She

A Generous Gift

Wilma was excited about the trip to Melbourne, Australia, for the 1956 Olympics, but she worried that she had nothing to wear. Her parents could not afford to buy the things she needed. But some people in the town of Clarksville called Coach Gray. They told him, "Bring Wilma downtown, let her buy some clothes and some luggage so she can go to Melbourne in style, and we'll take care of everything."[7]

Before she left town, the people put on a send-off party for their star runner. Wilma was grateful for the rest of her life. The townspeople's generosity meant that Clarksville was proud of her, and they supported her all the way to the Olympics.

A Sad Moment in Paradise

Wilma fell in love with Hawaii's tropical palm trees and ocean beaches. It seemed like paradise. But while shopping in Honolulu, she and her teammates were confronted by the ugliness of racial prejudice. A white woman walking her dog abruptly crossed the street when she saw the athletes in her path. She glared at them in disgust. The incident made Wilma sad. She realized that no matter what glory she and her friends achieved, some people would still treat them like dirt because of their skin color.

was too anxious. The other girls picked at her tray until the food was gone.

At the training camp in smoggy Los Angeles, Wilma met the Olympic team's coach, Nel Jackson. She was from the Tuskegee Institute and was the first black woman to coach the Olympic track team. Jackson, and not Temple, would be traveling with the team to Melbourne. Wilma enjoyed the training camp. She felt fit and strong and ready to run her races in the Olympics, the 200-meter dash and the 4x100-meter relay.

But the plane had two more stops on its way to Australia— first Hawaii and then Fiji. On the island of Fiji, Wilma was amazed to see an entire nation of black people, all speaking a different language.

That amazed me at the time, and it really got me to thinking about how many people live on this planet. . . . I began to realize that the world was bigger than Clarksville, or even Tennessee, and I said to myself, "You're lucky, you're luckier than all of the kids back home, because you're getting to see all of these things and they're not."[8]

Olympic Trials and Triumphs

At last they arrived in Melbourne, at the Olympic Village, where more than 3,000 Olympic athletes from 67 countries would live during the course of the Games. Over the next weeks, Wilma would make many new friends from different countries around the world.

One of the new friends was Australian runner Betty Cuthbert. Known as the Golden Girl for her golden hair and gold-medal-winning speed, Cuthbert was the best runner in Australia. She was favored to win the sprint events. At 18, she was only a few years older than Wilma and gave friendly advice. Cuthbert showed off her white, kangaroo-leather running shoes and told Wilma where she could buy a pair. The shoes were remarkably light and comfortable compared to the cow-leather shoes Wilma wore. But Cuthbert's shoes cost between 20 and 30 dollars, and Wilma could not afford them.

The day of the 200-meter trial race came, and Wilma was nervous. Coach Temple was not there, and

The opening ceremonies of the Summer Olympic Games in Melbourne, Australia, were held in November 1956.

she lacked confidence. She blocked out everything in her mind except winning. In the first qualifying heat, she took third place. In the second heat, she came in third again—but only the first two places qualified. Wilma was out. She had not been fast enough to run the 200-meter race in the Olympics. "How will I ever be able to face them again back home? I'm a failure," she thought.[9]

Over the next several days, Wilma watched as her Australian friend Cuthbert won gold in the 100-, 200-, and 400-meter races. Instead of being jealous, she became inspired. The next Olympics would be held in 1960. She had four years to get there. If she trained hard enough, she could win gold too.

Meanwhile, her Olympic dreams were not over for this year. She still had the 4x100-meter relay. Faggs ran first, passing the baton off to Margaret Matthews. Matthews handed the baton to Wilma. It was a smooth

The Olympic Village

One of the first things Wilma noticed about the Olympic Village was that it was racially integrated. Black and white athletes ate at the same tables and bunked in the same rooms. Seeing the races mingle together opened Wilma's eyes. She had grown up in the segregated South, but now she saw there was another way of living.

Willye White, one of Wilma's teammates, commented,

> I came out of the deep South, where it was total segregation. . . . Whites and blacks did not mix. When I went to Melbourne . . . I found that there was a different world.[10]

Wilma was amazed to see so many different kinds of people—Asian, African, Latino, and white—all together in one place, speaking different languages. All of them, it seemed, were fascinated by the United States and were just as curious about her as she was about them. Outside the Olympic Village, people clamored for autographs from the US team. Wilma and her teammates sometimes spent more than an hour signing autographs. For the first time, Wilma felt that nobody looked at her differently for being black. She was, simply, an American track star.

Olympic Medals

For each Olympic event, three medals are awarded. Gold is for first place, silver is for second place, and bronze is for third. But originally, when the modern Olympics began in 1896, there was no gold medal. The first-place finishers received a silver medal. Gold medals were introduced at the 1904 Olympic Games in St. Louis, Missouri. Today, the Olympic gold medals are not solid gold, but sterling silver covered with a thin layer of gold.

pass, and Wilma ran her leg of the relay at top speed. She handed the baton to Isabelle Daniels, who came in third—just fractions of a second behind the Australian and British runners. The four girls from Tennessee had won a bronze medal for the United States.

Wilma came home to Clarksville a hometown hero. At Burt High School, classes were canceled and a special assembly was called in her honor. Wilma passed her bronze medal around so her classmates could touch the Olympic award.

Betty Cuthbert, *right*, of Australia's team crossed the finish line to win the gold in the 4x100 relay. Britain's Heather Armitage, *left*, won the silver for her nation.

The US women's track team placed third in the 100-meter relay in the 1956 Olympics. *From left*, Margaret Matthews, Wilma Rudolph, Mae Faggs, and Isabelle Daniels hold their medals.

Challenge and Change

Wilma Rudolph became famous in her hometown of Clarksville, Tennessee, as an Olympic bronze medalist. Everyone looked at her differently. Some wanted to be her friend just because of her success. Others were jealous and made nasty comments such as, "She ain't so hot." Wilma remembered, "They either put you on a pedestal, or else they put you down. There was no in-between."[1]

That season, the Burt High School girls basketball team was one of the best in Tennessee's history. Wilma averaged more than 30 points per game, and her friend Nancy Bowen also excelled. The team was undefeated. The girls went on to the state tournament and won the championship. But as the crowd cheered, coach Clinton Gray shouted at Wilma for a mistake she had made near the end of the game. Wilma stormed into the locker room, angry and embarrassed. It seemed that everyone, even Coach Gray, expected Wilma to be perfect now that she was an Olympic athlete.

"Wilma was a tremendous basketball player, she scored 50 points in one game. If there had been scholarships to play basketball back in those days, she could've won a scholarship playing basketball just as well."[3]
—*Coach Ed Temple*

The track season was a disappointment too. None of the girls wanted to run against Wilma because they figured they had no chance. So Wilma won all her races that year without even working at it. Her favorite sport began to feel a little boring.

Wilma was proud of her success, but she disliked the pressure that it brought. It also made her feel isolated, or set apart, from the other kids. Luckily, she could always count on her boyfriend, Robert Eldridge, and her best pals, Bowen and Delma Wilkerson, to make her feel like the same old Wilma again.

An Unforgettable Night

Now in her junior year at Burt High, Wilma finally had the chance to go to the junior-senior prom. She and Robert were excited to attend the event in style.

Robert was the star of the football and basketball teams, and Wilma was the track and basketball standout. "We were like King and Queen," she remembered.[2]

Wilma borrowed a blue evening dress from her friend Shirley Crowder, a student at Tennessee State.

She tried it on, and the dress was beautiful. Robert came to pick her up in his father's new car, a blue Ford. The two expected to have a night they would never forget.

The prom was held at the high school gym. After the dance had ended, some of the kids drove up to Hopkinsville, Kentucky, to a nightclub. "Last one to Hopkinsville is a chicken!" they shouted.[4] They raced to Hopkinsville, speeding all the way. Later that night, they raced each other home. Robert and Wilma were two of the first to get back, and Wilma spent the night at her friend Delma's house.

Around four in the morning, Coach Gray called Delma's house, frantically looking for Wilma. When she came to the phone, he was crying. "Thank God you're alive," he said.[5] He shared some

Teen Driving Risks

Motor vehicle crashes are the most common cause of death for US teenagers. Drivers aged 16 to 19 are four times more likely than older drivers to crash. Risk factors include using cell phones, talking to other passengers, speeding, and drinking alcohol.

terrible news. Wilma's friend Nancy had been in a car wreck on the way home from Hopkinsville. The driver had been racing with the others at high speed and smashed into a concrete pillar. Nancy and the driver were killed instantly. Coach Gray had thought Wilma was in the car too.

Wilma was in shock. Nancy had been her close friend for years, and now she was dead at 16. Wilma returned to Nashville that summer to train with the Tigerbelles, but it was difficult for her to concentrate on running. "Nancy's death was my first experience with tragedy. I couldn't handle it. I was an emotional

Teen Pregnancy in the 1950s

In the 1950s, teen pregnancy was a cause for shame. Young girls who became pregnant were often sent away to live with another family member until their babies could be given up for adoption. Sometimes they were expelled from school. For Wilma, it was not so bad. Although she felt embarrassed by her condition, she was not the only pregnant girl at Burt High School. She was allowed to finish high school and keep her child.

Sex education was not provided in most schools in the 1950s, and parents often avoided speaking to their children about sex. The lack of education meant that the teen pregnancy rate was higher in the 1950s than it is today. In Wilma's case, her parents were religious Southern Baptists.

"I couldn't ask about such things as sex, because sex was a taboo subject in the religion," Wilma wrote in her autobiography. "A lot of things I wanted to know more about back then, and I should have been able to go to my mother for the answers. But I never did."[6]

wreck for weeks," Wilma recalled in her autobiography. "To this day, I hear the word 'prom' and feel bad."[7]

Another Shock

As Wilma began her senior year in high school, her future looked bright. She had won a track scholarship to Tennessee State University. As long she kept her grades up and ran for the Tigerbelles, she would attend classes for free. The little girl who had once been kept home from school with a damaged leg would now be the first in her family to attend college. Wilma was also in top physical shape. She had already won a bronze medal at the Olympics, and she looked forward to going for the gold in three years.

But as she prepared for a new track season, she received a shock. Dr. Coleman, after giving her a yearly physical, informed Wilma that she was pregnant. Wilma could not believe it. She and Robert were in love, and they had just begun to experiment with sex. They knew nothing about birth control and never thought this could happen.

Wilma wanted to have the baby, but she knew her parents, her coaches, and the whole town would be disappointed in her—an Olympic athlete pregnant at 17. She kept her condition a secret for weeks. At last, Coach Gray noticed her thickening waist during basketball practice and guessed what was happening.

A Secret Visitor

Wilma's boyfriend, Robert, was not permitted to come to the house—not even to meet baby Yolanda. But one night that summer while everyone was asleep, Wilma heard a rapping at the window. At first, she was afraid someone was trying to break in. Then she saw it was Robert, coming for a glimpse of his daughter. She opened the window and held Yolanda up for him to see.

"You're pregnant, Wilma, and it's serious," he said. "You're going to have a baby, and you need to talk to your parents about this. This is more important than basketball."[8]

Wilma's parents were supportive. "Don't be ashamed of anything," her father said. "Everybody makes mistakes."[9] But Ed Rudolph made one thing clear: He did not want his daughter to see Robert again.

As Wilma's pregnancy progressed, she hung up her basketball and track shoes for the rest of the year. She graduated from Burt High in June 1958. In July, Wilma had a baby girl and named her Yolanda.

With a baby, it looked as if Wilma's career as a track star might be over. Coach Temple had a rule that no mothers were allowed on his track team. But to Wilma's delight, the coach made an exception. Beginning that fall, she would be a Tigerbelle. Wilma's sister Yvonne offered to care for baby Yolanda while Wilma started college. Everything was falling into place.

Wilma Rudolph in 1961

CHAPTER 7

Dorothy Hyman, Wilma Rudolph, and Jutta Heine after the 200-meter race at the 1960 Olympics in Rome, Italy

Going for Gold

In September of 1958, Wilma Rudolph began school at Tennessee State, majoring in elementary education with a minor in psychology. She had to study hard because coach Ed Temple required his athletes to maintain a B-average. Meanwhile, she worked two hours a day on campus and ran track with the Tigerbelles. The schedule was exhausting.

Rudolph began to have doubts. She missed her baby. Also, Robert Eldridge, who had managed to stay in contact with her against her father's wishes, had been hinting that she should drop out of school and quit track. She could marry him and be a stay-at-home wife and mother. One day, she talked to her history teacher, Mr. Knight, about her dilemma. He advised her not to quit. She had worked very hard at running to get to where she was now. And Yolanda was well taken care of. She could stay in school and compete in track and still be a good mother to her daughter. "Wilma, you *can* have both," he said.[1]

Rudolph knew her teacher was right. Getting an education was important, and she did not want to quit running and give up her Olympic dream. There would be time later to be a wife and full-time mother. But still, that night, she went back to her room and cried.

Off to Rome

Rudolph kept working and training hard. In the summer of 1960, she broke the world record in the 200-meter dash with a time of 22.9 seconds. She easily qualified for the Olympics in the 100- and 200-meter dashes and in the 4x100-meter relay at the Olympic trials. At the end of August, she was headed to Rome, Italy, for the 1960 Summer Olympic Games. Along with her were Tigerbelles teammates Lucinda Williams, Barbara Jones, and Martha Hudson. The four made up the fastest relay team the United States had to offer.

A Young Mother's Scare

Over Christmas 1958, Rudolph received a scare. Her sister Yvonne, who had been caring for baby Yolanda for five months, wanted to adopt the baby. Rudolph panicked. She found Eldridge, and the two hatched a plan. In the middle of the night, they drove all the way to Yvonne's house in St. Louis, Missouri. They snatched the baby, then drove back. When they got home, Rudolph's father was furious. But he calmed down when he saw the baby. "This baby ain't going nowhere," he said. "It's staying right here."[2] After that, Rudolph's parents cared for Yolanda in Clarksville.

To Rudolph, Rome was like "a storybook city come true." The ancient Roman Colosseum, the underground catacombs, and the Roman Catholic holy city of the Vatican were all around, "like . . . pictures come to life."[3] The Italians were friendly. And the other athletes at the Olympic Village were friendly too. They wanted the American girls to teach them the latest dance moves.

Rudolph felt relaxed and ready to run. But a day or two before she was scheduled to run her first qualifying race, something unfortunate happened. While jogging through a sprinkler to cool off during a training exercise, she stumbled into a small hole, straining her ankle. The ankle immediately swelled and became discolored, and Rudolph began to cry. Would this injury derail her Olympic dreams? All she could do was allow the trainers to wrap her ankle tightly, ice it, and rest it as much as possible before her first race.

"Most people don't realize that you work a lifetime to run 9, 10, 11 seconds, and you can't plan for it. No matter how many years you train to try to become the best, at that point, anybody in the race has the same chance. You just can't plan it. It is being mentally tough. And it takes a very special person to be mentally tough for 9 seconds."[4]
—*Wilma Rudolph, in* Runner's World, *1993*

"Vil-ma! Vil-ma!"

It was a swelteringly hot 100 degrees Fahrenheit (37.78°C), and 80,000 spectators were packed into the *Stadio Olimpico* in Rome. Rudolph listened for the announcer to call her name for the 100-meter dash. She propped her feet up against the wall and hoped her ankle would be okay. At least she would not have to run around any curves in the 100-meter dash. When she heard her name, Rudolph walked calmly through the tunnel and into the stadium. The Italian crowd roared, chanting, "Vil-ma, Vil-ma!" Rudolph put all other thoughts aside. She was here to win.

Rudolph's ankle injury did not slow her down. She won her qualifying race in 11 seconds flat—another world record, although officials did not count it because there had been a

"The '60 Olympics was my greatest thrill. And when I think back on it, I still get frightened, to remember a capacity crowd in the stadium all standing and chanting my name."[5]
—*Wilma Rudolph*

strong wind at her back. Soon after, Rudolph qualified for the 200-meter dash as well. She was on to the finals.

It was the moment for which Rudolph had been waiting. She stood in the tunnel, glancing at the other five runners. Among the top runners were Giuseppina Leone of Italy and Dorothy Hyman of Great Britain. Then there was Jutta Heine, a tall, blond German sprinter. Rudolph worried most about Heine. At five feet, 11 inches (1.8 m), Rudolph counted her height as an advantage. She was not sure how she would do against a runner like Heine, who was just as tall. But she convinced herself not to worry. After all, she was the one with the world-record time.

"I compare it to a jet engine taking off: It's on the runway, engines racing. Then it takes off on a slant and goes up gradually."[6]

—*Coach Ed Temple, describing the 100-meter start*

The runners emerged from the tunnel. Camera bulbs flashed. Reporters noted that Rudolph, the favorite, was running on a taped and bandaged ankle. Would the record-breaking Tennessee star be able to perform?

The 100-meter dash gold-medal winner Rudolph, *center*, with silver medalist Hyman, *left*, and bronze medalist Leone, *right*

The gun went off. The runners leapt out of the blocks in unison, but Rudolph soon pulled to the front. Head back, arms pumping, Rudolph crossed the finish line three yards (2.74 m) ahead of the next runner—it was not even close. Again, she had run the race in the world-record time of 11 seconds. Again, the superfast time could not be officially counted in the record books because she had been aided by the wind. But she had won without any doubt. Rudolph stepped up onto the winner's box and received her first gold medal.

Three Gold Medals

Rudolph had won her first gold medal, but she had two more events to run. She hoped to have three gold medals by the time she left Italy. Next up was the 200-meter race. Rudolph again faced Heine and Hyman, whom she had defeated in the 100-meter dash.

The runners blasted around the curve, accelerating to nearly 20 miles (32.2 km) an hour. Rudolph ran on the inside lane, moving up steadily. On the stretch, she took the lead. Leaning forward and her legs moving fluidly, she seemed to fly over the track. Rudolph outpaced all the other runners, breaking the tape four yards (3.66 m) ahead of the second-place finisher, Heine. Rudolph was disappointed with her time of 24 seconds. She knew she could do better—she had already run it in 22.9 seconds during practice and trials, setting a world record, and in 23.2 seconds in the first qualifying heat, setting an Olympic record. But 24 seconds was still fast, and it earned Rudolph her second gold medal.

Rudolph's last event was the 4x100-meter relay. She was running the final leg of the race—the anchor leg. When it was her turn, she started running, stretching her arm backward to receive the baton from teammate Williams. The pass was a bad one, and Rudolph almost dropped the baton. Had she dropped it,

Rudolph runs in a 200-meter qualifying heat at the 1960 Olympics.
She finished in 23.2 seconds, a Games record.

the team would have been disqualified. She held onto it, but now she was way behind.

She saw Heine ahead of her. She was used to pushing herself to the limit in order to win, and she really wanted to win this one for her teammates. Rudolph poured on the speed, passing Heine and a Soviet runner and came in first. She and her teammates won gold with a world-record time of 44.5 seconds.

Rudolph made history as the first American woman to win three gold medals in a single Olympic Games.

Fastest Woman on Earth

As Rudolph stepped down from the stand, she was mobbed by reporters. Everyone was fascinated with her story. The press dubbed her the Tennessee Tornado and the World Speed Queen. The French called her *La Perle Noire*, or the Black Pearl, while the Italians nicknamed her *La Gazzella Nera*, or the Black Gazelle. Years later, Rudolph remembered:

> *They called me the "Black Gazelle" in Rome, and I thought that was wonderful. I didn't find it offensive at all, because I knew they weren't just speaking of color. They were speaking of something beautiful in color and motion.*[7]

Olympic Flubs

Although Olympic relay teams practice passing the baton many hundreds of times before a race, mistakes can occur in an instant that destroy their hopes for Olympic glory. At the 2008 Summer Olympics in Beijing, both the US men's and women's 4x100-meter relay teams dropped the baton and were disqualified. Both times, the baton was dropped while the third runner handed it to the fourth and final runner.

"*I can't* are two words that have never been in my vocabulary. I believe in myself more than anything else in this world."[8]
—*Wilma Rudolph*

Rudolph would never forget the 1960 Olympic Games in Rome. From now on, the world would not forget Rudolph either. If her speed was thrilling, her story was inspiring. She had overcome poverty, racism, and disability to become the fastest woman on Earth.

Rudolph displays the three gold medals she won in the 1960 Olympics.

Rudolph and her parents ride in a parade held in Rudolph's honor in Clarksville, Tennessee, after the 1960 Olympics.

A Sweet Taste

"Wilma, life will never be the same for you again," warned an Olympic official after Wilma Rudolph won her third gold medal.[1] He was right. Rudolph was now an international star. Everyone wanted to see her run. So instead of returning home after the Games, Rudolph and the other three Tigerbelles spent several weeks running races all over Europe. Everywhere they went, fans and reporters mobbed Rudolph. In Germany, someone even stole her track shoes as a souvenir.

Rudolph's teammates became jealous. They also had earned Olympic gold but were getting no attention. One night, the three girls hid a set of hair curlers from Rudolph as she was getting ready for an awards banquet. Rudolph had to attend the banquet with messy hair. Coach Ed Temple, furious, scolded the girls for their nasty trick.

Rudolph was happy when it was time to return to Clarksville, Tennessee. Little did she know what a grand homecoming it would be. The town of

40,000 people came out to see her, and a victory parade was held in her honor. Rudolph rode in a car with her mother and her father, waving at the people who lined the streets. She also noted something very special about the event. In the crowd, she saw black faces and white faces. It was the town's first racially integrated public event. On that day, Rudolph's success had broken down racial barriers in her hometown. Later, she participated in public protests against segregation until the racist laws were no more.

Running against Sexism

Rudolph's Olympic success not only helped break down racial barriers, but gender barriers as well. In the 1960s, some Americans still believed that sports were for men. *New York Times* sportswriter Arthur Daley complained in an article published during the 1960 Olympic Games,

> *It just doesn't seem right to watch a female leap clumsily over the bars, throw the weights awkwardly or scamper over a track in unladylike fashion. They lose all their daintiness and appeal.*[2]

But Rudolph's victories made women's track popular in the United States and showed that running was not only a man's sport. In February 1961, Rudolph was invited to participate in the prestigious Millrose Games in New York City. In 30 years, no woman had run in the event. But that year, a special 60-yard (54.86-m) sprint was organized just for Rudolph. She ran it in 6.9 seconds, tying her own world-record time.

Rudolph was proud to be the first woman to run in many races that had previously been all-male events, including the New York Athletic Club meet, the *Los Angeles Times* runs, and the Penn Relays at the University of Pennsylvania in Philadelphia.

Impressing the President

While in Washington DC for a track meet in April 1961, Rudolph had the honor of meeting President John F. Kennedy at the White House. Rudolph was very nervous. "What do you say to the President of the United States . . . Hello?"[3] she wondered. Just after they had posed for photographs together, Kennedy went to sit back down in his chair—and missed. He fell onto the floor. "It's not every day that I get to meet an Olympic champion," he joked. Rudolph relaxed, and they talked for about half an hour. "It's really an honor to meet you and tell you what a magnificent runner you are," Kennedy said.[4]

That month, Rudolph experienced loss as well. Her father, Ed, passed away due to complications from diabetes.

"Wilma had a smile and personality that won over queens and common folk. She toured the continent, and everybody wanted to see her, including the Queen of England. At the White House, Jack Kennedy was so taken that he almost missed his rocking chair when he tried to sit down in the Oval Office. I saw that. He almost fell down."[5]

—*Coach Ed Temple*

Rudolph, invited to meet with President Kennedy, chats at the White House in April 1961.

He had been ill for some time with the disease. Rudolph's father had supported her dreams. She was sad he was gone but glad he had lived to share in her victory.

Also in 1961, Rudolph married fellow Tennessee State athlete William Ward. The marriage did not work out, and it ended in 1962.

Time to Retire

Rudolph won many awards after her Olympic triumphs in 1960. That year, she was named Athlete of the Year by the United Press. The Associated Press honored her as Woman Athlete of the Year for 1960 and 1961. Also for 1961, Rudolph won the James E. Sullivan Award, the most prestigious award given to amateur athletes. And in 1962, she received the Babe Didrikson Zaharias Award for outstanding female athlete.

Rudolph wondered whether it might be time to retire. The Olympics were coming up in 1964. But if she ran and failed to win gold in all her events again, people might remember her failure and forget her success. "You lose in 1964, and that's what people will remember—the losses, not the three golds in 1960," Coach Temple cautioned her.[6]

Babe Didrikson Zaharias

Mildred "Babe" Didrikson Zaharias (1911–1956) is known as one of the greatest female athletes who ever lived. Didrikson won two gold medals and one silver medal in track and field at the 1932 Los Angeles Olympics. She also excelled at basketball, baseball, softball, diving, and bowling. In her later years, she became famous as an expert golfer. Like Wilma Rudolph after her, Didrikson helped break down stereotypes about women. When asked by a reporter whether there was anything she did not play, Didrikson quipped, "Yeah, dolls."[7]

Rudolph was honored by the AAU (Amateur Athletic Union) with the 1961 James E. Sullivan Award.

In July 1962, Stanford University in northern California held a meet between Soviet and US runners. At that time, the Soviet Union and the United States were rival superpowers, pitted against each other in the Cold War. Rudolph looked forward to beating the Soviet team. When the day came, she sprinted to victory in the 100-meter race and zoomed past her Soviet rival in the last leg of the 400-meter relay. As she remembered it:

> *I caught her, I passed her, and won. . . . The crowd in the stadium was on its feet, giving me a standing ovation, and I knew what time it was. Time to retire, with a sweet taste.*[8]

Afterward, Rudolph spent an hour signing autographs. When she had finished, she sat on a bench to remove her track shoes. Just then, a young boy approached and asked shyly,

The Cold War

The Cold War (1947–1991) was a rivalry that occurred after World War II between the Soviet Union and its allies and the United States and its allies. The nations had different ideologies and political systems. The competition for supremacy was called the Cold War because it did not lead to direct fighting between the superpowers. The Cold War, however, dominated US and Soviet foreign policy from the late 1940s until the collapse of the Soviet Union in 1991.

Retirement Age

Twenty-two might seem like a young age for retirement. Female runners today often continue into their late thirties or even beyond. Olympian Gail Devers competed at the Millrose Games in 2007 at age 40—and ran the fastest time of anyone that year in the 60-meter hurdles. However, when Rudolph was running, there were far fewer opportunities for female track and field athletes. "If Wilma was coming along now, she'd be still running. . . . She wasn't close to her peak. But there was nothing out there then," commented coach Ed Temple in an interview in 1994.[10]

"Miss Rudolph . . . can I please have your autograph?" Rudolph smiled. "Son . . . I'll do better than that," she said.[9] She signed her track shoes and gave them to the astonished boy. She never ran a race again.

Rudolph won two events in a US-Soviet meet in 1961 in Moscow. A year later, another US-Soviet meet would be the final event of her career.

CHAPTER 9

Rudolph graduated from college on May 27, 1963.

Life after Track

Wilma Rudolph graduated from Tennessee State with a degree in elementary education. She had retired from running but continued promoting sports and physical education. In May 1963, she traveled to Africa as a Goodwill Ambassador for the US State Department. She attended the Games of Friendship, a track and field event in Senegal. Later, she went to Japan with evangelist Billy Graham as a member of the Baptist Christian Athletes.

Although she now traveled around the world, she had not forgotten her friends in Clarksville. She often visited coach Clinton Gray at Burt High School. Sometimes she would surprise him, coming up behind him to cover his eyes and ask, "Guess who?" But when she returned from Japan in 1963, she did not find Gray at the school. Tragically, he had just been killed in a car accident.

Rudolph was deeply saddened by the loss of her old friend and mentor. Several months later, Burt High School asked Rudolph if she would

Protesting Segregation

While in Clarksville in the early 1960s, Rudolph participated in public protests against segregation. In 1963, she and other black community leaders attempted, time and again, to enter whites-only restaurants in town. Eventually, Clarksville's restaurants were forced to change their rules and admit black people.

Rudolph was greatly affected by the 1968 assassination of Martin Luther King Jr. Shortly after his death, she was at a bus station in Nashville when a white man spat at her children. The police were called, and the man was arrested. Rudolph wondered whether things would ever change.

take Gray's job as the girls track coach. She was honored to do so. Rudolph also began teaching second grade at Cobb Elementary, her former school. Now she was doing two things she loved—teaching and coaching. They allowed her to give back to her community by passing on what she had learned from Coach Gray, coach Ed Temple, and her teachers and mentors throughout the years.

Time for a Family

Having found work in Clarksville, Rudolph felt ready to settle down. In 1963, she married Robert Eldridge. They had three more children. A daughter, Djuana, was born in 1964. In 1965, she gave birth to a boy, Robert Jr. In 1971, Rudolph's second son, Xurry, was born. Her oldest daughter, Yolanda, became involved in running. Eventually, she attended Tennessee State and became a Tigerbelle like her mother. Rudolph encouraged Yolanda to run for the love of it and not to worry about living up to the Rudolph name.

Although happy with her growing family, Rudolph lacked money. Today, Olympic athletes are paid thousands of dollars to run races or endorse products. Olympic runner Marion Jones became a millionaire after winning gold in the 2000 Olympics. But in the 1960s, such opportunities did not exist for runners, especially not black female runners. "If you thought about it negatively, you could get angry," Rudolph said.[1]

"You become world famous and you sit with kings and queens, and then your first job is just a job. You can't go back to living the way you did before because you've been taken out of one setting and shown the other. That becomes a struggle and makes you struggle."[2]
—*Wilma Rudolph, talking to* Ebony *magazine in 1984*

Exploring New Career Paths

Rudolph loved teaching, but she was frustrated at Cobb Elementary. She had new ideas, but the teachers and administrators at the school wanted to do everything the same way it had always been done. Rudolph quit, taking a job in Evansville, Indiana, as director of a community center. Later, she moved to Poland Springs, Maine, to work in a youth recreation program.

In 1967, Hubert H. Humphrey, the vice president of the United States, recruited Rudolph for Operation Champion, a new program to train young athletes living in the ghettos of the nation. Rudolph loved the job. Although she was from a smaller town and the kids she trained were from city neighborhoods, she could relate to them. Like Rudolph years before, they needed encouragement to reach for big dreams. Rudolph welcomed another opportunity to pass on what her teachers and coaches had taught her to a new generation of African-American young people.

Rudolph worked in California, then in Chicago for Mayor Richard J. Daley's Youth Foundation. Tall and beautiful, Rudolph even found work as a fashion model. While many employers hired her for her famous name, they did not want to hear her ideas. She felt used. In the late 1970s, Rudolph formed her own company, Wilma Unlimited. She chose the name because she did not want to be limited in what she could do. As she was finding a new path in her work life, she also made a change in her personal life. Rudolph and her husband, Robert, divorced in 1976.

In 1982, Rudolph and her children moved to Indianapolis, Indiana. The previous year, she formed the Wilma Rudolph Foundation to help amateur athletes. "[H]ave confidence in yourself. Triumph can't be had without a struggle," she reminded the athletes.[3]

Honors and Struggles

Rudolph was voted into the Black Athletes Hall of Fame in 1973 and the National Track and Field Hall of Fame in 1974. She was inducted into the US Olympic Hall of Fame in 1983 and the National Women's Hall of Fame in 1994. But her financial struggles continued. In the late 1990s, she filed for bankruptcy.

"No one has a life where everything that happened was good," Rudolph once said. "I think the thing that made life good for me is that I never looked back. I've always been positive no matter what happened."[4]

Her Toughest Race

In 1994, Rudolph learned she was suffering from brain cancer. She kept a positive attitude, hoping to fight it and win. But the cancer spread too quickly. A few months after her diagnosis, 54-year-old Rudolph died at her home in Nashville.

Wilma

In 1977, Rudolph reflected on her life in an autobiography, *Wilma*. It was made into a television movie starring Cicely Tyson as Blanche Rudolph and Denzel Washington as Robert Eldridge.

Rudolph is shown with her family and an unidentified guest, *top left*, in 1976.

The state of Tennessee went into mourning for Rudolph. In the days after her death, state flags were flown at half-mast. A memorial service was held at Kean Hall at Tennessee State University, where Rudolph's track career had blossomed with Coach Temple and the Tigerbelles. A funeral was held at First Baptist Church in Clarksville, where young Wilma had first walked down the aisle without her leg brace. Nearly 2,000 mourners gathered in Clarksville to remember Rudolph, the Olympic champion, the Tennessee Tornado.

"Wilma was the most sharing person I ever coached," Temple reflected.[5] He added that she had taken more joy in winning the relay for her teammates than in her other gold medals. Rudolph had shared her wisdom and experience with a new generation of athletes. As she put it, "I have spent a lifetime trying to share what it has meant to be a woman first in the world of sports so that other young women have a chance to achieve their dreams."[6]

Leaving a Legacy

Rudolph broke down gender and race barriers in sports. She proved that a woman could be

Sprint Speed Records

Rudolph set a world record in the 200-meter dash, running that distance in 22.9 seconds. Her time of 11 seconds in the 100-meter dash would have been a world record, but it was considered wind-aided. The 4x100-meter Olympic team anchored by Rudolph set a world-record time of 44.5 seconds.

As of 2010, the world records for the 100- and 200-meter dash were held by Florence Griffith Joyner. She set them, respectively, at the Olympic trials and the Olympic Games in 1988. She ran the 100-meter race in an astonishing 10.49 seconds. Her time in the 200-meter dash was 21.34 seconds.

feminine and graceful and still burn up the track. She came from a racially segregated town, but her victory brought her town together, black and white, in jubilant celebration. She paved the way for African-American female track and field athletes who came after her, including Jackie Joyner-Kersee, Florence Griffith Joyner (Flo-Jo), and Gail Devers. She watched Flo-Jo capture gold medals in the 100- and 200-meter dashes in the 1988 Olympics in Seoul, South Korea. But she also inspired many more humble athletes through her work with the Wilma Rudolph Foundation.

In 1996, a statue of Rudolph was put up in Clarksville. It shows Rudolph in mid-stride, as she looked while crossing the finish line in Rome in 1960.

It is a familiar pose copied from photographs of the event. Head back, body extended toward the tape, the figure of Wilma Rudolph looks like the image of strength, determination, and grace in motion.

"Wilma Rudolph's courage and her triumph over her physical handicaps are among the most inspiring jewels in the crown of Olympic sports. . . . She was speed and motion incarnate, the most beautiful image ever seen on the track."[7]
—*Jesse Owens, African-American track star and hero of the 1936 Olympic Games*

Rudolph, *right*, with Florence Griffith Joyner, who won the 100- and 200-meter races in the 1988 Olympics

TIMELINE

1940

Wilma Glodean Rudolph is born on June 23 in St. Bethlehem, Tennessee.

1944

Rudolph becomes sick with polio, which paralyzes her left leg.

1952

Rudolph is able to walk without a leg brace at age 12.

1958

In July, Rudolph gives birth to her first child, daughter Yolanda.

1960

Rudolph competes at the Olympic Games in Rome, Italy, winning three gold medals.

1961

Rudolph runs the 60-yard dash in 6.9 seconds at the Millrose Games, tying her own world record.

1956

Rudolph attends a summer training camp for runners at Tennessee State University.

1956

In November, Rudolph competes at the Olympic Games in Melbourne, Australia, winning a bronze medal in the 4x100-meter relay.

1958

Rudolph graduates from high school and wins a full scholarship to Tennessee State.

1961

Rudolph is named Woman Athlete of the Year by the Associated Press.

1961

Rudolph receives the James E. Sullivan Award.

1961

Rudolph meets President John F. Kennedy.

1962

After winning two races at a US-Soviet track meet, Rudolph retires from racing at age 22.

1962

Rudolph wins the Babe Didrikson Zaharias Award as the most outstanding female athlete.

1963

On May 27, Rudolph graduates from Tennessee State with a degree in elementary education.

1974

Rudolph is voted into the National Track and Field Hall of Fame.

1977

Rudolph publishes her autobiography, *Wilma*, which will later be made into a television film.

1981

Rudolph establishes the Wilma Rudolph Foundation to help young athletes.

1963

Rudolph marries high school sweetheart Robert Eldridge.

1963

Rudolph begins teaching at Cobb Elementary School and coaching track at Burt High School.

1967

Rudolph is recruited for the Operation Champion program.

1983

Rudolph is inducted into the US Olympic Hall of Fame.

1994

Rudolph is inducted into the National Women's Hall of Fame.

1994

On November 12, Rudolph dies at home in Nashville, Tennessee, after a battle with brain cancer.

DATE OF BIRTH
June 23, 1940

PLACE OF BIRTH
St. Bethlehem, Tennessee

DATE OF DEATH
November 12, 1994

PARENTS
Ed and Blanche Rudolph

EDUCATION
Cobb Elementary School and Burt High School in Clarksville, Tennessee; Tennessee State University in Nashville

MARRIAGES
William Ward (1961–1962)

Robert Eldridge (1963–1976)

CHILDREN
Yolanda, Djuana, Robert Jr., Xurry (all with Eldridge)

CAREER HIGHLIGHTS

Wilma Rudolph set Olympic world records as a sprinter. At her peak, she was known as the fastest woman in the world. She captured a bronze medal at the 1956 Melbourne Olympics for the women's 4x100-meter relay and three gold medals at the 1960 Olympics in Rome, one each for the 100-meter race, 200-meter race, and 4x100-meter relay.

SOCIETAL CONTRIBUTIONS

Rudolph paved the way for female athletes by being the first woman to run in previously all-male events. Her success as an African American helped break down racist attitudes in America and abroad. After the 1960 Olympics, Rudolph's hometown of Clarksville, Tennessee, hosted its first racially integrated parade in her honor. Rudolph promoted athletics for underprivileged youth through the Wilma Rudolph Foundation.

CONFLICTS

When she was four, Rudolph's left leg became partially paralyzed from polio. As a result, she was unable to walk without a brace until age 12. She overcame her physical limitations to become the fastest woman in the world. Rudolph grew up in a poor black family in the segregated South yet became a hero of her town.

QUOTE

"I believe in me more than anything in this world."
—*Wilma Rudolph*

GLOSSARY

amateur
An athlete who is not paid to compete in sports.

barrier
Something standing in the way of progress or freedom.

baton
The hollow stick passed between runners during a relay race.

epidemic
A disease that affects a large percentage of a community.

heat
A race held at the beginning of a meet to determine who will go on to the final race.

ideologies
Systems of ideas or beliefs.

immunize
To make someone resistant to a disease.

integrated
Not segregated; open to people of all races.

mentor
A teacher or guide.

orthopedic
Having to do with muscles and bones.

ovation
Cheering and clapping by an audience.

physical therapy
The treatment of muscles or bones with massage, exercise, or heat.

prestigious
Important or highly respected.

qualify
To reach a standard that allows a person to advance to the next level.

relay
A race between teams in which each member of the team completes part of the distance.

segregation
The separation of people of different races or religions.

sprint
A short race run at top speed.

taunt
To make fun of someone.

vaccine
An injection or pill that can protect a person against a particular disease.

welfare
A government program that aids people with little money.

SELECTED BIBLIOGRAPHY

"Ahead of Their Time." *Runner's World*, June 1993, Vol. 28, No. 6.

Biracree, Tom. *Wilma Rudolph: Champion Athlete*. New York: Chelsea House Publishers, 1988.

Rudolph, Wilma. *Wilma: The Story of Wilma Rudolph*. New York: New American Library, 1977.

FURTHER READINGS

Christopher, Matt. *The Olympics: Unforgettable Moments of the Games*. New York: Little, Brown & Co., 2008.

Harper, Jo. *Wilma Rudolph: Olympic Runner*. New York: Aladdin Paperbacks, 2004.

Sherrow, Victoria. *Wilma Rudolph*. Minneapolis, MN: Carolrhoda Books, 2000.

WEB LINKS

To learn more about Wilma Rudolph, visit ABDO Publishing Company online at **www.abdopublishing.com**. Web sites about Rudolph are featured on our Book Links page. These links are routinely monitored and updated to provide the most current information available.

PLACES TO VISIT

The National Women's Hall of Fame
76 Fall Street, Seneca Falls, NY 13148
315-568-8060
www.greatwomen.org
As of 2010, Wilma Rudolph was one of 236 American women honored in the National Women's Hall of Fame. The hall is in Seneca Falls, New York, known as the birthplace of women's rights.

US Olympic Visitor Center
1750 East Boulder Street, Colorado Springs, CO 80909
888-659-8687
http://teamusa.org/about-usoc/colorado-springs-olympic-training-ctr/tours.html
Visitors can take a free tour of athlete-training facilities, learn about Olympic athletes past and present, and visit the US Olympic Hall of Fame Rotunda and the US Olympic Store.

Wilma Rudolph Statue
College Street and Riverside Drive, Clarksville, TN 37040
A bronze statue of Wilma Rudolph stands in her hometown of Clarksville, Tennessee. It honors Rudolph as one of America's greatest Olympic athletes.

CHAPTER 1. The Fastest Woman on Earth

1. Wilma Rudolph. *Wilma: The Story of Wilma Rudolph.* New York: New American Library, 1977. Print. 121.
2. *American Women of Achievement: Wilma Rudolph.* Prod. and Dir. Wolfington Productions, Inc. Schlessinger Video Productions, 1995. Videocassette.
3. Wilma Rudolph. *Wilma: The Story of Wilma Rudolph.* New York: New American Library, 1977. Print. 121.
4. Ibid. 124.

CHAPTER 2. Beating the Odds

1. Wilma Rudolph. *Wilma: The Story of Wilma Rudolph.* New York: New American Library, 1977. Print. 18.
2. Ibid. 8.
3. Ibid. 5.
4. Tom Biracree. *Wilma Rudolph.* New York: Chelsea, 1988. Print. 32.
5. Wilma Rudolph. *Wilma: The Story of Wilma Rudolph.* New York: New American Library, 1977. Print. 31.
6. Ira Berkow. "Wilma Rudolph Obituary: Forever the Regal Champion." *New York Times.* New York Times Company, 13 Nov. 1994. Web. 29 Nov. 2010.
7. Wilma Rudolph. *Wilma: The Story of Wilma Rudolph.* New York: New American Library, 1977. Print. 22.
8. Ibid. 11.
9. Ibid. 32.
10. Ibid. 19.

CHAPTER 3. Becoming an Athlete

1. Wilma Rudolph. *Wilma: The Story of Wilma Rudolph.* New York: New American Library, 1977. Print. 43.
2. Ibid. 49.
3. Ira Berkow. "Wilma Rudolph Obituary: Forever the Regal Champion." *New York Times.* New York Times Company, 13 Nov. 1994. Web. 29 Nov. 2010.
4. Wilma Rudolph. *Wilma: The Story of Wilma Rudolph.* New York: New American Library, 1977. Print. 56.
5. Ibid. 63.

6. Ibid. 65–66.

CHAPTER 4. Toughening Up

1. Alex Haley. "The Queen Who Earned Her Crown." *The Unlevel Playing Field: A Documentary History of the African American Experience in Sport.* Ed. David K. Wiggins and Patrick B. Miller. Urbana: U of Illinois P. Print. 266.

2. Wilma Rudolph. *Wilma: The Story of Wilma Rudolph.* New York: New American Library, 1977. Print. 70.

3. *American Women of Achievement: Wilma Rudolph.* Prod. and Dir. Wolfington Productions, Inc. Schlessinger Video Productions, 1995. Videocassette.

4. Wilma Rudolph. *Wilma: The Story of Wilma Rudolph.* New York: New American Library, 1977. Print. 71.

5. Ibid. 71.

6. Ibid. 69–70.

7. Ibid. 72.

8. Ibid. 75–76.

9. Ibid. 77.

10. Ibid. 79.

CHAPTER 5. To the Olympics

1. *American Women of Achievement: Wilma Rudolph.* Prod. and Dir. Wolfington Productions, Inc. Schlessinger Video Productions, 1995. Videocassette.

2. "Ahead of Their Time." *Runner's World* June 1993. *Gale Biography in Context.* Web. 29 Nov. 2010.

3. Wilma Rudolph. *Wilma: The Story of Wilma Rudolph.* New York: New American Library, 1977. Print. 84.

4. "Double Sprint Champion Hurries Only on Track." *New York Times* 6 Sept. 1960: 44. Print.

5. *American Women of Achievement: Wilma Rudolph.* Prod. and Dir. Wolfington Productions, Inc. Schlessinger Video Productions, 1995. Videocassette.

6. Wilma Rudolph. *Wilma: The Story of Wilma Rudolph.* New York: New American Library, 1977. Print. 84.

7. Ibid. 85.

8. Ibid. 90.

9. Ibid. 96.

10. "Ahead of Their Time." *Runner's World* June 1993. *Gale Biography in Context.* Web. 29 Nov. 2010.

CHAPTER 6. Challenge and Change

1. Wilma Rudolph. *Wilma: The Story of Wilma Rudolph.* New York: New American Library, 1977. Print. 104.

2. Ibid. 105.

3. *American Women of Achievement: Wilma Rudolph.* Prod. and Dir. Wolfington Productions, Inc. Schlessinger Video Productions, 1995. Videocassette.

4. Wilma Rudolph. *Wilma: The Story of Wilma Rudolph.* New York: New American Library, 1977. Print. 106.

5. Ibid. 107.

6. Ibid. 12–13.

7. Ibid. 108.

8. Ibid. 110.

9. Ibid. 111.

CHAPTER 7. Going for Gold

1. Wilma Rudolph. *Wilma: The Story of Wilma Rudolph.* New York: New American Library, 1977. Print. 119.

2. Ibid. 117.

3. Ibid. 126.

4. "Ahead of Their Time." *Runner's World* June 1993. *Gale Biography in Context.* Web. 29 Nov. 2010.

5. Ira Berkow. "Forever the Regal Champion." *New York Times.* New York Times Company, 13 Nov. 1994. Web. 29 Nov. 2010.

6. "Lauryn Williams Is Keeping Fast Company." *USA Today* 24 Aug. 2004: 04F. Print.

7. "Ahead of Their Time." *Runner's World* June 1993. *Gale Biography in Context.* Web. 29 Nov. 2010.

8. "Great Olympic Moments." *Ebony* Jan. 1992. *Google Book Search.* Web. 29 Nov. 2010.

CHAPTER 8. A Sweet Taste

1. Wilma Rudolph. *Wilma: The Story of Wilma Rudolph.* New York: New American Library, 1977. Print. 136.

2. Arthur Daley. "In Praise of Greeks." *New York Times* 9 Sept. 1960: 20. Print.

3. Wilma Rudolph. *Wilma: The Story of Wilma Rudolph.* New York: New American Library, 1977. Print. 149.

4. Ibid. 150.

5. "Long Legs, Wide Smile, Big Heart." *Newsweek* 25 Oct. 1999: 55. Print.

6. Tom Biracree. *Wilma Rudolph: Champion Athlete.* New York: Chelsea, 1988. Print. 93.

7. Matt Christopher. *The Olympics: Unforgettable Moments of the Games.* New York: Little Brown, 2008. Print. 29.

8. Wilma Rudolph. *Wilma: The Story of Wilma Rudolph.* New York: New American Library, 1977. Print. 153.

9. Ibid. 153.

10. *American Women of Achievement: Wilma Rudolph.* Prod. and Dir. Wolfington Productions, Inc. Schlessinger Video Productions, 1995. Videocassette.

CHAPTER 9. Life after Track

1. "Ahead of Their Time." *Runner's World* June 1993. *Gale Biography in Context.* Web. 29 Nov. 2010.

2. "Whatever Happened to Wilma Rudolph?" *Ebony* Feb. 1984. *Google Book Search.* Web. 29 Nov. 2010.

3. M. B. Roberts. "Rudolph Ran and World Went Wild." *ESPN. com.* ESPN Internet Ventures, n.d. Web. 29 Nov. 2010.

4. "Whatever Happened to Wilma Rudolph?" *Ebony* Feb. 1984. *Google Book Search.* Web. 29 Nov. 2010.

5. "Long Legs, Wide Smile, Big Heart." *Newsweek* 25 Oct. 1999. Print. 58.

6. Marney Rich Keenan. "Wilma Rudolph: 'It's Important to Be Yourself and Have Self-Confidence.'" *Chicago Tribune* 8 Jan. 1989. *Pro Quest.* Web. 29 Nov. 2010.

7. "Wilma Rudolph." *Contemporary Heroes and Heroines.* Vol. 2. Detroit: Gale, 1992. *Biography Resource Center.* Web. 5 Nov. 2010.

Amateur Athletic Union meets, 31, 39–42
Anderson, Annette, 38
Associated Press Woman Athlete of the Year, 81

Babe Didrikson Zaharias Award, 81
Berlin, Germany, 12
Black Athletes Hall of Fame, 91
Bowen, Nancy, 28, 57, 60
Burt High School, 26, 29, 54, 57–59, 60, 61, 62, 87

Clarksville, Tennessee, 18, 20, 29, 49, 51, 54, 57, 66, 77, 87–88, 92–93, 94
Cobb Elementary, 21, 29, 88, 89–90
Coleman, Dr., 15, 61
Crowder, Shirley, 58
Cuthbert, Betty, 51, 53

Daniels, Isabelle, 45, 54
Devers, Gail, 84, 94

Eldridge, Djuana (daughter), 88
Eldridge, Robert (husband), 31, 40, 58–59, 61, 62, 65, 66, 88, 90
Eldridge, Robert, Jr. (son), 88
Eldridge, Xurry (son), 88

Faggs, Mae, 46–49, 53

Gray, Clinton, 26–28, 31, 40, 49, 57, 59–61, 87–88

Heine, Jutta, 69, 71–72
Hopkinsville, Kentucky, 59–60
Hudson, Martha, 38, 47, 66
Hyman, Dorothy, 69, 71

Jackson, Nel, 50
James E. Sullivan Award, 81
Jones, Barbara, 8, 36, 66
Jones, Marion, 89
Joyner, Florence Griffith, 93, 94
Joyner-Kersee, Jackie, 94

Kennedy, John F., 79

Leone, Giuseppina, 69

Melbourne, Australia, 8, 45, 48–53

Nashville, Tennessee, 19, 20, 22, 32, 35, 60, 88, 91
National Track and Field Hall of Fame, 91
National Women's Hall of Fame, 91
Newcombe, Don, 42

Olympic Games,
  1936, 10, 12, 94
  1956, 8–9, 45, 48–54
  1960, 7, 11, 66–74, 81
  history, 9
  medals, 9–11, 12, 38, 46, 53, 54, 57, 61, 70–73, 77, 81–89, 93
  Olympic Village, 51, 53, 67
  relay events, 9, 11, 12, 46, 50, 53–54, 66, 71, 73, 93

sprint events, 9–11, 51, 53, 68–71, 93
Olympic Hall of Fame, US, 91
Olympic trials
1956, 45–48
1960, 7, 10–11, 66
Operation Champion, 90
Owens, Jesse, 9–10, 12

polio, 12, 16–17

Robinson, Jackie, 42
Rome, Italy, 7, 11, 66–74, 94
Rudolph, Blanche (mother), 15–20, 22, 25–26, 35, 60, 66, 78
Rudolph, Ed (father), 17–18, 26, 62, 65, 66, 78, 79–80
Rudolph, Wilma,
    awards and honors, 81, 91
    basketball, 7, 25–31, 32, 57–58, 61–62
    birth, 15
    childhood, 15–32
    death, 91–92
    education, 20–21, 29, 31, 58, 62, 65–66, 87
    illnesses, 15–16
    leg brace, 20–22, 93
    marriages, 80, 88
    nicknames, 28, 73
    Olympic medals, 9, 11, 54, 57, 61, 70–73, 77, 93
    polio treatment, 17, 18, 19–22
    prom, 58–61
    retirement, 81–84
    teen pregnancy, 61–62

world records, 7, 9, 11, 15, 66, 68–72, 78, 93
Rudolph, Yolanda (daughter), 62, 65, 66, 88–89
Rudolph, Yvonne (sister), 26, 62, 66

segregation, 15, 20, 21, 29, 42, 53, 78, 88, 94
sexism, 26, 78
St. Bethlehem, Tennessee, 15

Temple, Ed, 7–8, 11, 32, 35–36, 37, 38–39, 40, 45, 48–49, 50, 51, 58, 62, 65, 69, 77, 79, 81, 84, 88, 92–93
Tennessee A&I State University, 7, 8, 11, 32, 35, 38, 41–42, 49, 58, 61, 62, 65, 66, 77, 89, 92
Tigerbelles, 7, 11, 32, 35, 36, 38, 40, 45, 60, 61, 62, 65, 66, 77, 89, 92
Tuskegee Institute, 31–32, 50

Ward, William (husband), 80
White, Willye, 38, 53
Wilkerson, Delma, 58–59
Williams, Lucinda, 66, 71
Wilma Rudolph Foundation, 91, 94
Wilma Unlimited, 90

Youth Foundation, 90

Zaharias, Mildred "Babe" Didrikson, 81

ABOUT THE AUTHOR

Jennifer Joline Anderson has been writing since she was a teenager when she won a contest and had her first short story published in *Seventeen* magazine. Today, she lives in St. Paul, Minnesota, where she writes and edits books for young people.

PHOTO CREDITS